PEOPLE IN MY NEIGHBORHOOD

THE DENTIST

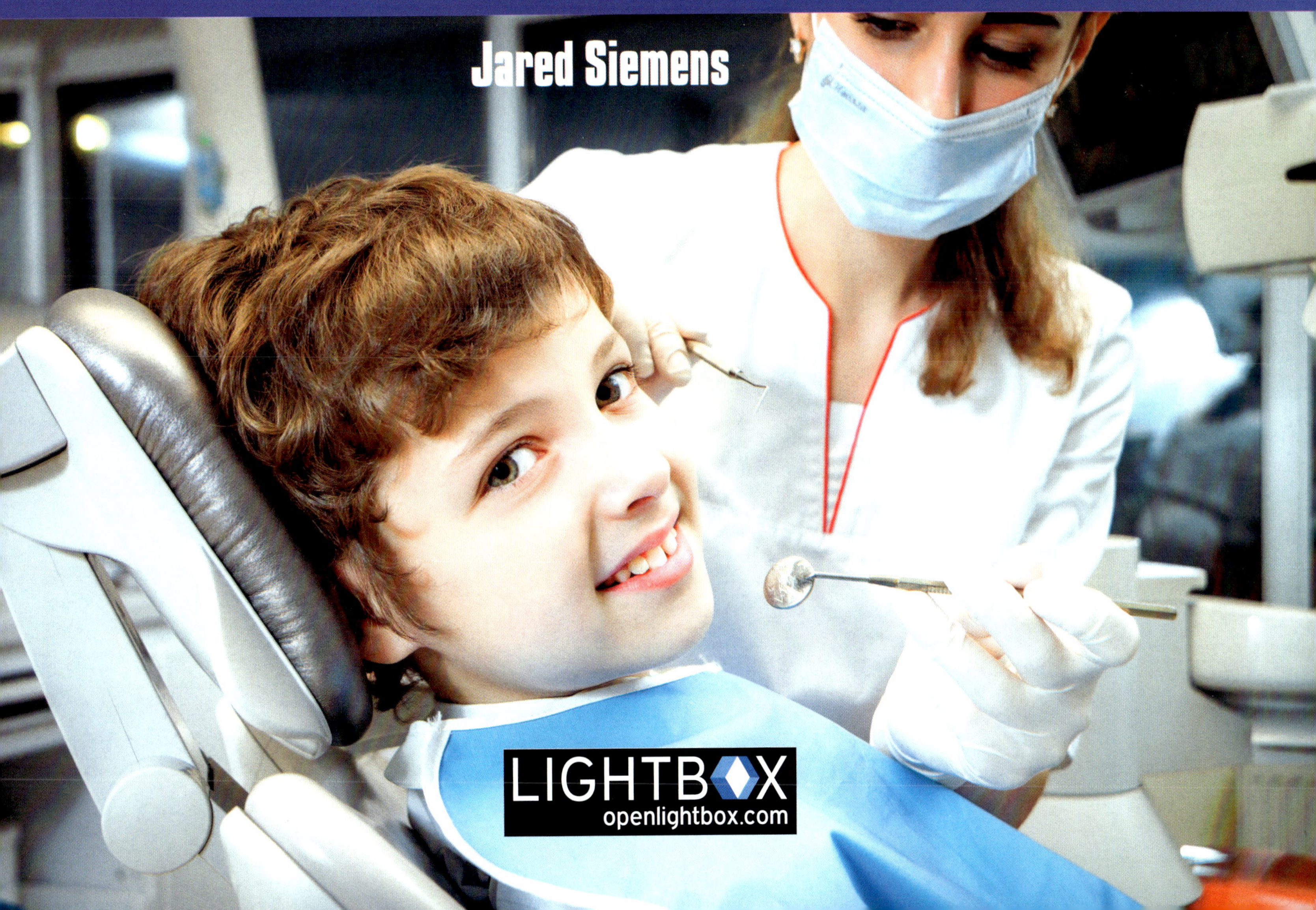

Jared Siemens

LIGHTBOX
openlightbox.com

LIGHTBOX

Go to **www.openlightbox.com** and enter this book's unique code.

ACCESS CODE

LBXJ4399

Lightbox is an all-inclusive digital solution for the teaching and learning of curriculum topics in an original, groundbreaking way. Lightbox is based on National Curriculum Standards.

OPTIMIZED FOR

- ✓ **TABLETS**
- ✓ **WHITEBOARDS**
- ✓ **COMPUTERS**
- ✓ **AND MUCH MORE!**

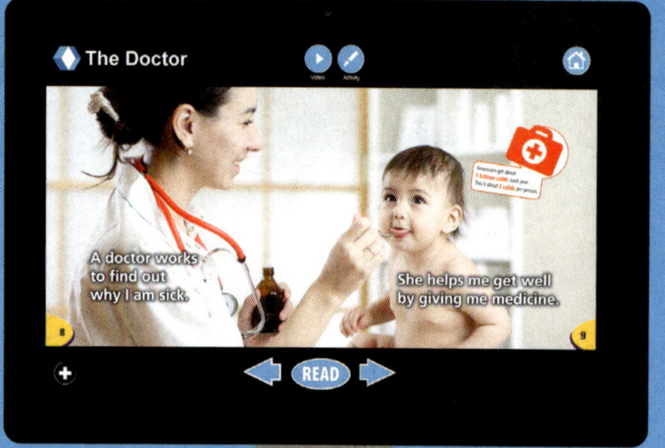

STANDARD FEATURES OF LIGHTBOX

 **AUDIO** High-quality narration using text-to-speech system

 **VIDEOS** Embedded high-definition video clips

 **ACTIVITIES** Printable PDFs that can be emailed and graded

 **WEBLINKS** Curated links to external, child-safe resources

 **SLIDESHOWS** Pictorial overviews of key concepts

 **INTERACTIVE MAPS** Interactive maps and aerial satellite imagery

QUIZZES Ten multiple choice questions that are automatically graded and emailed for teacher assessment

 **KEY WORDS** Matching key concepts to their definitions

VIDEOS

WEBLINKS

SLIDESHOWS

QUIZZES

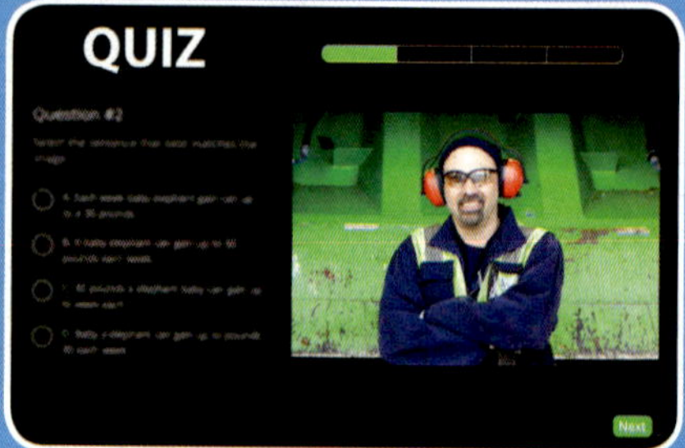

PEOPLE IN MY NEIGHBORHOOD

THE DENTIST

CONTENTS

There are many different people in my neighborhood.

The dentist is a person in my neighborhood.

The dentist works at a dental office.

A dental office is a place where people have their teeth checked.

A dentist helps people care for their teeth.

There are more than **180,000** dentists in the **United States**.

She makes sure that my teeth and gums are healthy.

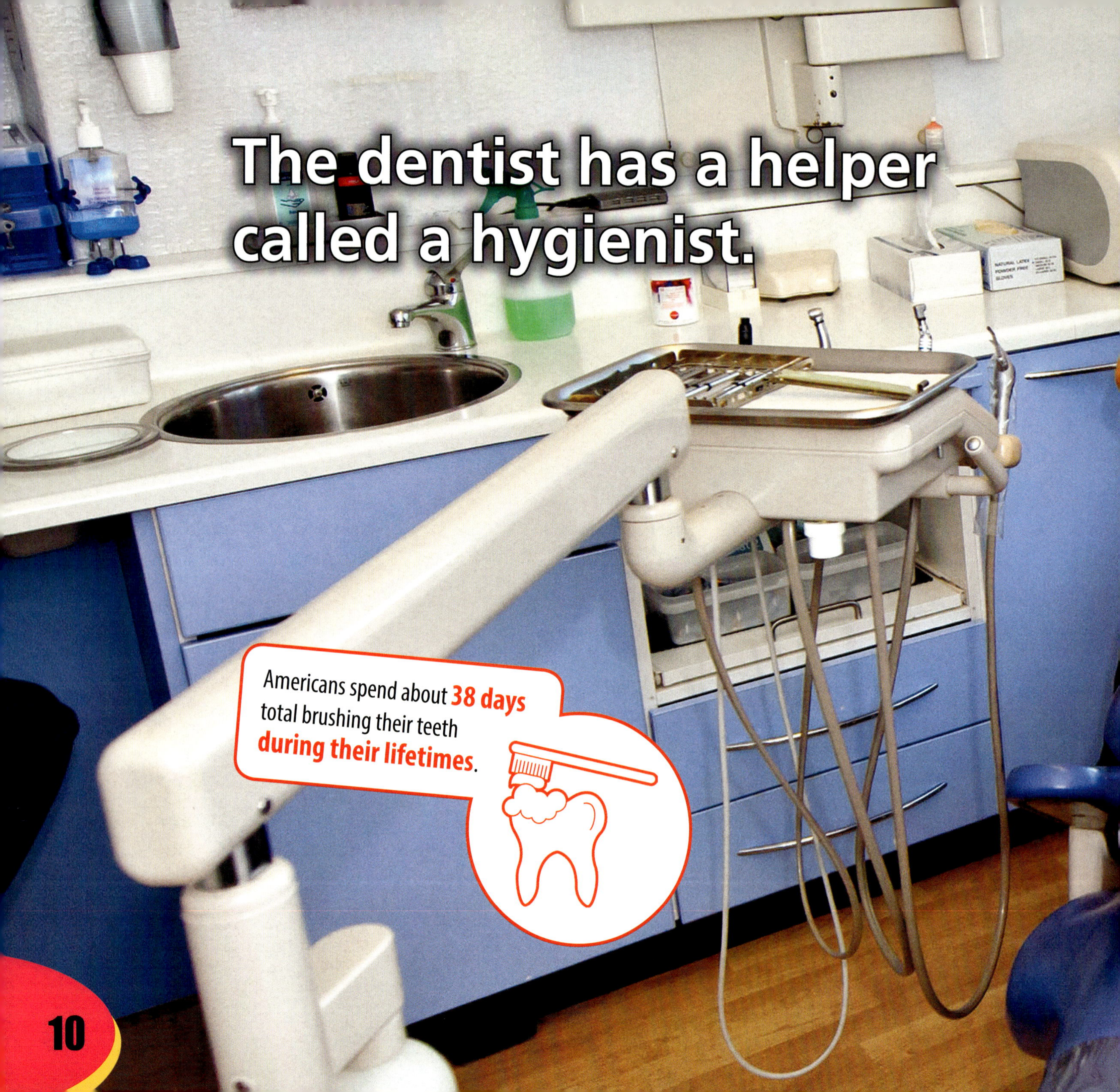

The dentist has a helper called a hygienist.

Americans spend about **38 days** total brushing their teeth **during their lifetimes**.

She cleans and
flosses my teeth.

The hygienist uses a bright light to see inside my mouth.

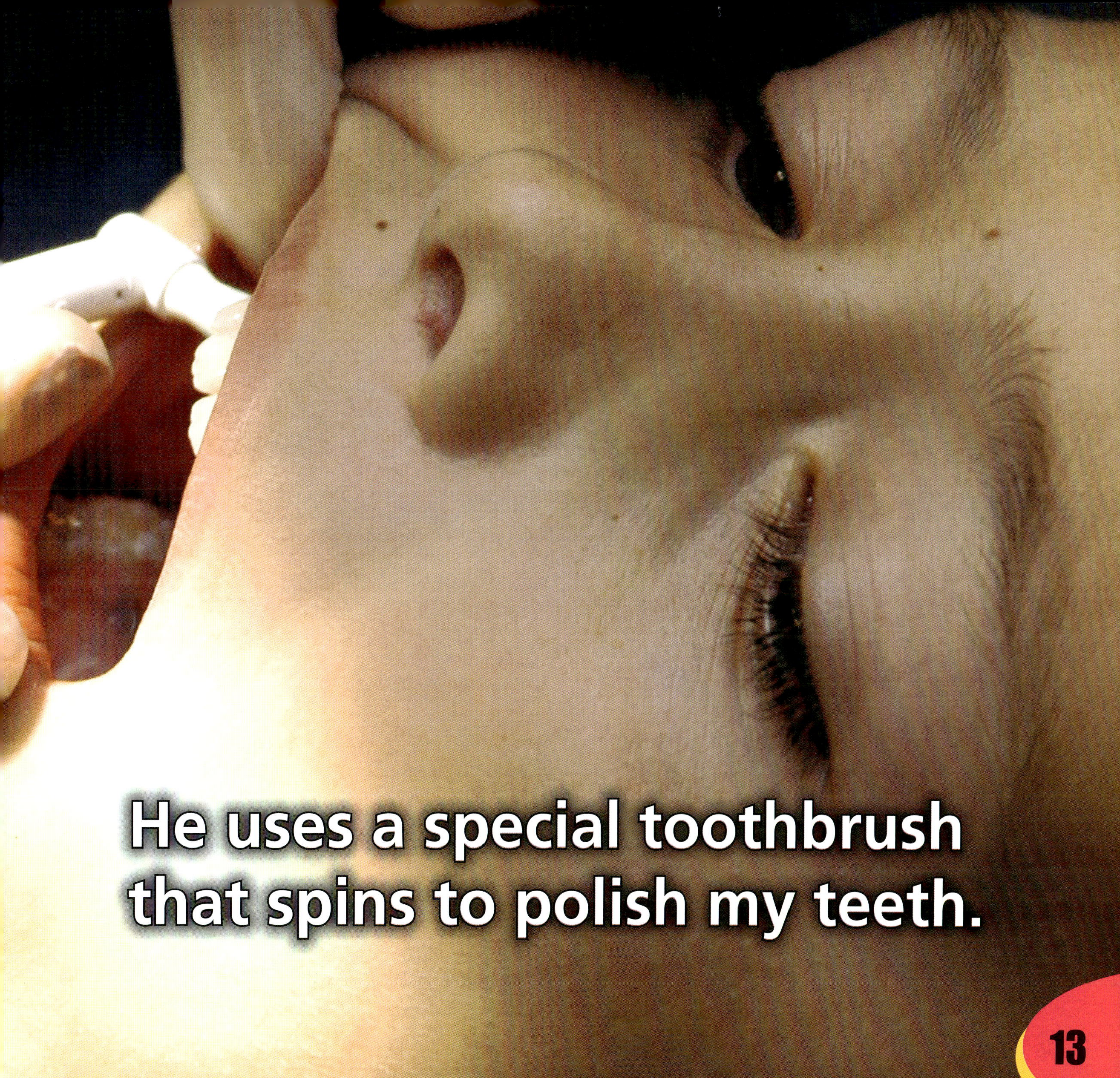

He uses a special toothbrush that spins to polish my teeth.

The dentist takes pictures of my teeth with an X-ray machine.

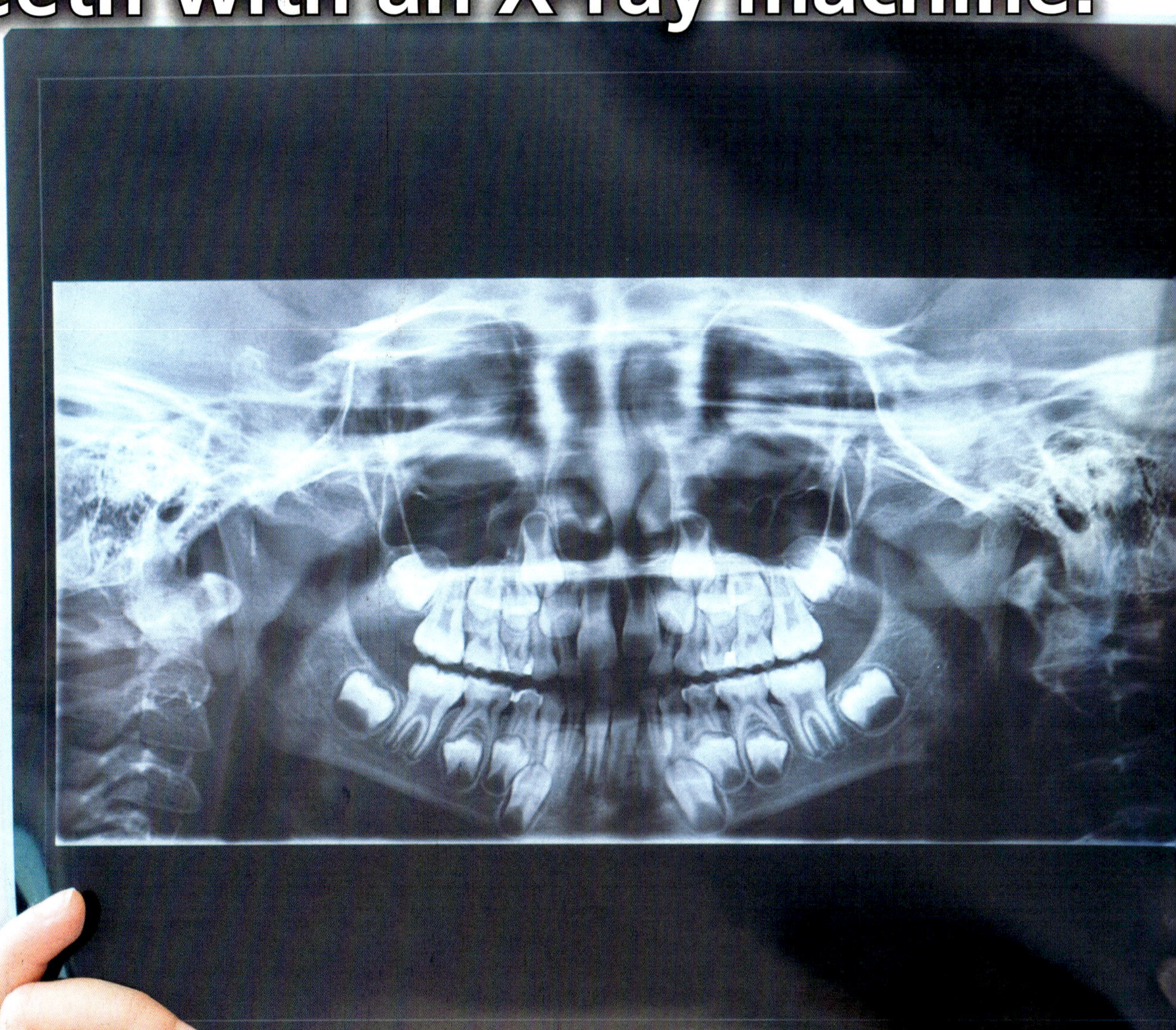

These pictures help the dentist see if my teeth are healthy.

A hole in a tooth is called a cavity.

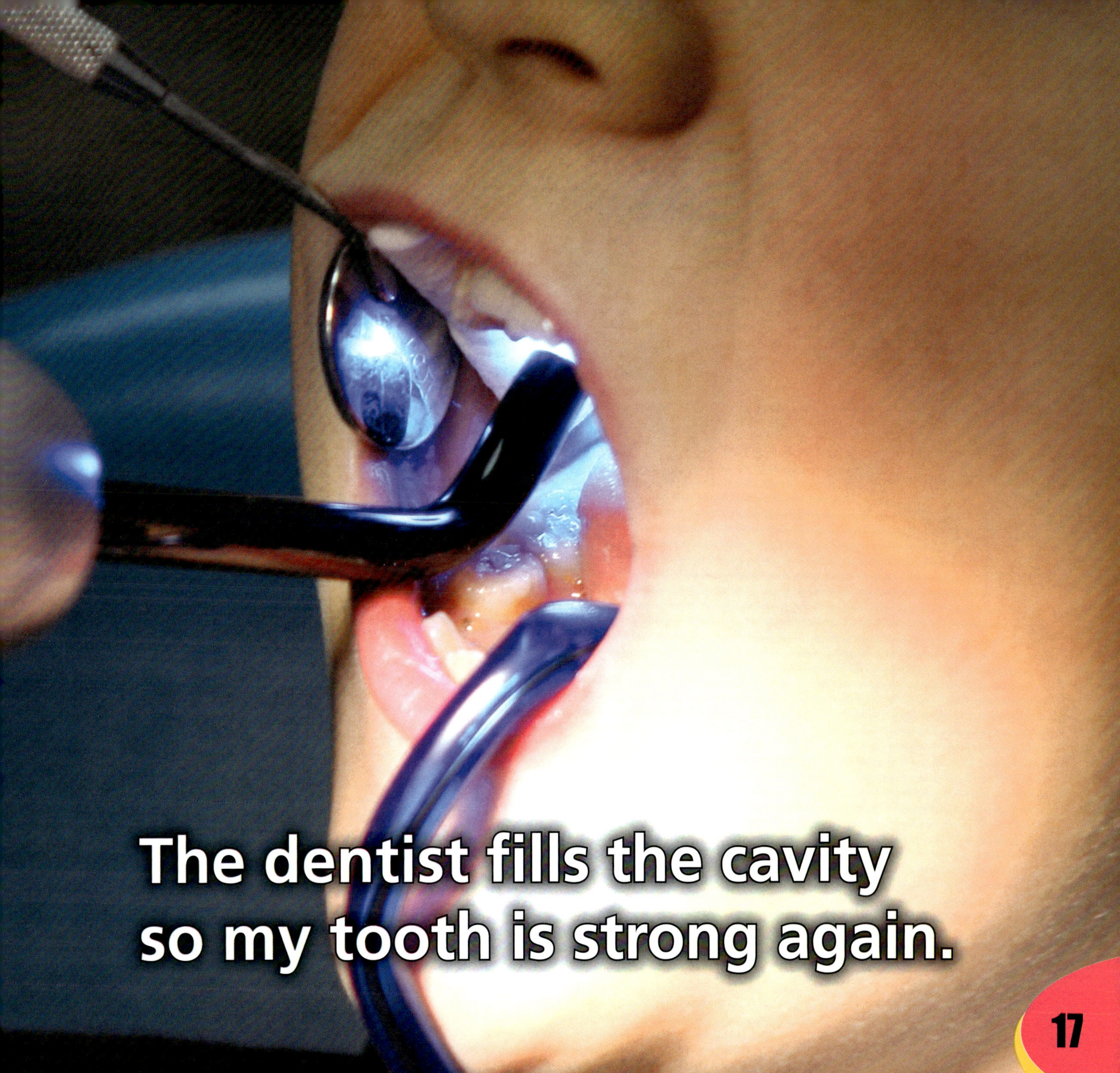

The dentist fills the cavity so my tooth is strong again.

The dentist shows me how to brush and floss my teeth.

Brushing and flossing keep my teeth strong and healthy.

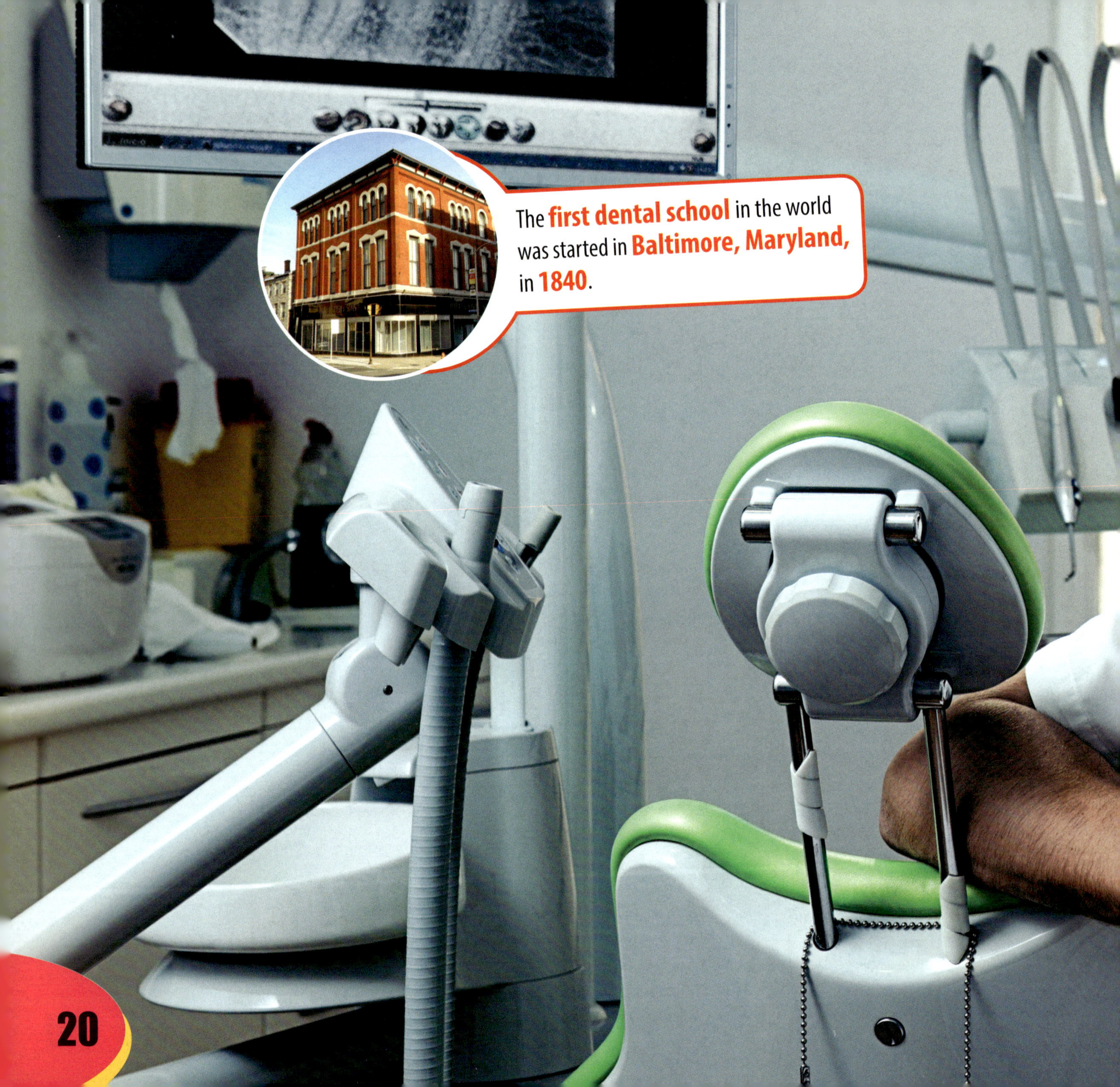

The **first dental school** in the world was started in **Baltimore, Maryland,** in **1840**.

Dentists are important people in my neighborhood.

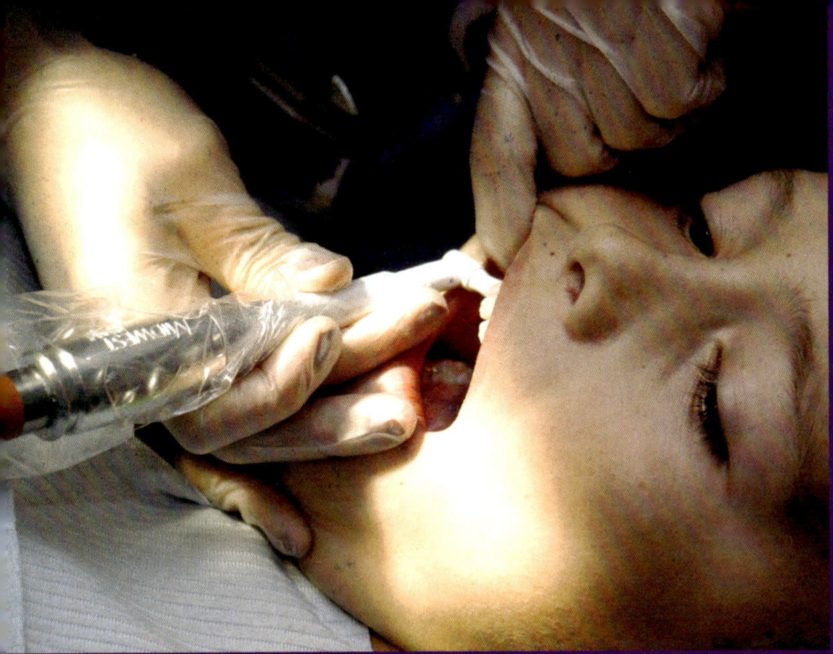

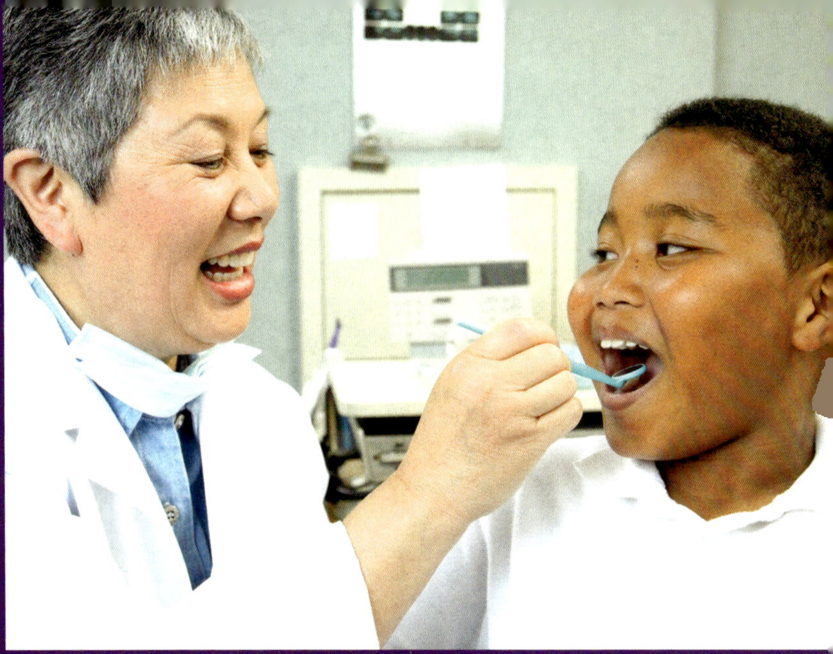

See what you have learned about the dentist and hygienist.

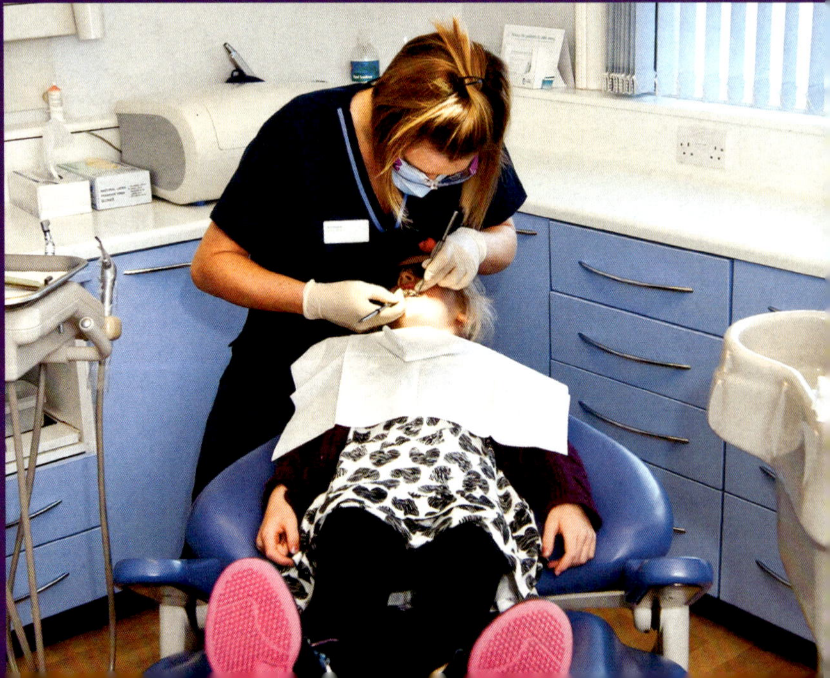

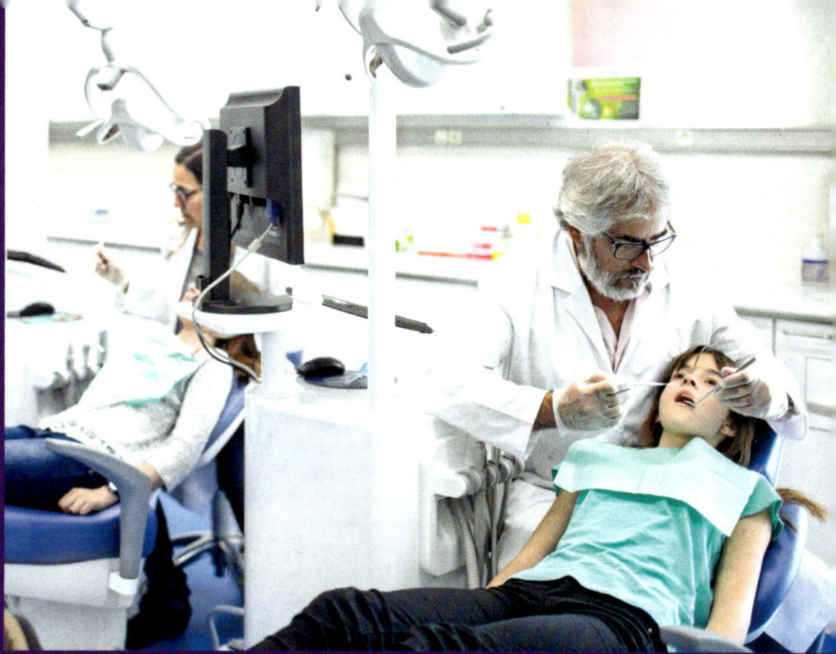

Describe what you see in each of the pictures.

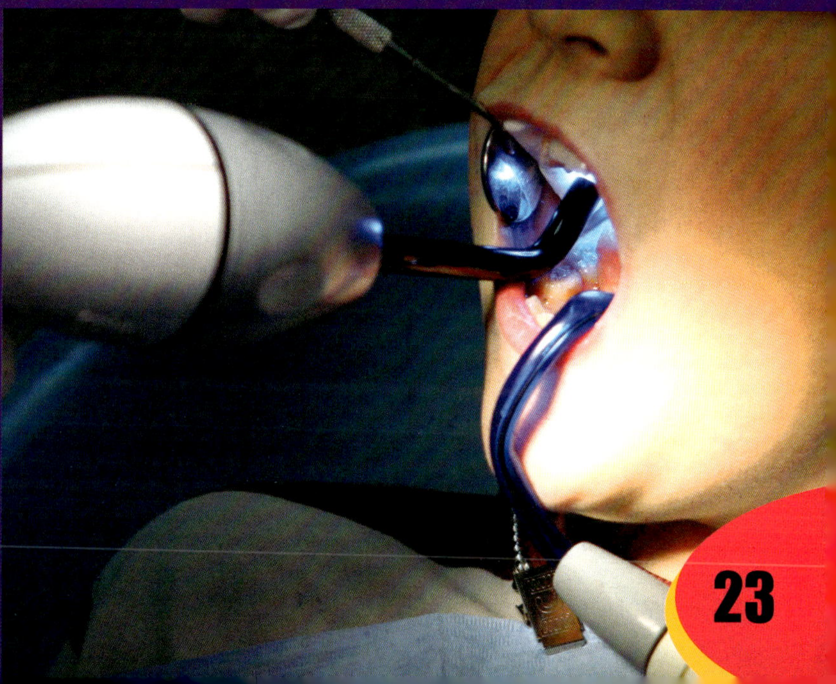

KEY WORDS

Research has shown that as much as 65 percent of all written material published in English is made up of 300 words. These 300 words cannot be taught using pictures or learned by sounding them out. They must be recognized by sight. This book contains 57 common sight words to help young readers improve their reading fluency and comprehension. This book also teaches young readers several important content words, such as proper nouns. These words are paired with pictures to aid in learning and improve understanding.

Page	Sight Words First Appearance
4	are, different, in, many, my, people, there
5	a, is, the
6	at, works
7	have, place, their, where
8	for, helps, more, states, than
9	and, makes, she, that
10	about, Americans, days, has
12	light, see, to, uses
13	he
14	an, of, pictures, takes, with
15	if, these
16	by, most, one, will
17	again, so
18	how, me, shows
19	keep
20	first, school, started, was, world
21	important

Page	Content Words First Appearance
4	neighborhood
5	dentist, person
6	dental office
7	teeth
8	United States
9	gums
10	helper, hygienist
12	mouth
13	toothbrush
14	X-ray machine
16	cavity, hole, tooth
20	Baltimore, Maryland

Published by Smartbook Media Inc.
350 5th Avenue, 59th Floor New York, NY 10118
Website: www.openlightbox.com

Library of Congress Control Number: 2018930446

ISBN 978-1-5105-3825-2 (hardcover)
ISBN 978-1-5105-3826-9 (multi-user eBook)

032018
120117

Printed in Brainerd, Minnesota, United States
1 2 3 4 5 6 7 8 9 0 22 21 20 19 18

Project Coordinator: Jared Siemens
Designer: Nick Newton

Every reasonable effort has been made to trace ownership and to obtain permission to reprint copyright material. The publisher would be pleased to have any errors or omissions brought to its attention so that they may be corrected in subsequent printings.

The publisher acknowledges Alamy, Shutterstock, Getty Images, iStock, and Wikimedia Commons as its primary image suppliers for this title.